Brain
purging pain
through poetry)

Melanie Bull

BookLeaf
Publishing
India | USA | UK

Brain Farts (purging pain through poetry)
© 2024 Melanie Bull

All rights reserved.

Melanie Bull asserts the moral right to be
identified as author of this work.

Presentation by *BookLeaf Publishing*

Web: www.bookleafpub.com

E-mail: info@bookleafpub.com

ISBN: 9789358316292

First edition 2024

ACKNOWLEDGEMENT

I would like to thank two of my best friends Kim Allibone and Michelle Parry that have always encouraged me to follow my dreams and inspired me.

My daughter Chloe bull, and grandchildren Ella, Ollie for giving me unconditional love and support and being my number one fans.

My mum and Dad for always encouraging me to pursue my poetry dreams

And lastly and not least my partner Andrew Knight for listening to every piece of poetry I write sharing the emotional challenges I faced.

The Tree of Life

The branches have fallen the tree is bare.
It feels unloved like nobody cares
It wants to have it confidence back
But without that mindset this it lacks.
All will be okay with some TLC
The Tree will return where it needs to be.
Plenty of sunshine and plenty of rain
Will help it return to it's old self again.
The branches with grow and the leaves will
return.
The gorgeous colours of green and auburn
The flowers will bloom and look a beautiful
sight.
And the tree will blossom from day to night.
We all fall apart at times but fight your way
back.
Focus, take a minute get back on track.
Sometimes it just takes some self care. or a
reassuring friend to say they will be there.
You too like the tree will stand tall and proud.
Now take a look in that mirror and say I've got
this out loud! ♥♥♥

Positivity

I'm on a journey of highs and lows
How long it will take nobody knows
I want to look in the mirror and like what I see
Because I hate the reflection staring back at me.
I want to walk down the street without feeling
insecure
I want to dance the night away and not feel a
bore.
I know I can do it I just hate feeling this way
It makes me feel like hiding away.
But I will get there and achieve the new me
So any of you doubters you will see.
I will look in the mirror and smile at me.

My Endo fight

I'm trying hard to win this fight
But it' gets exhausting every night
Just a few days without pain to be able to sleep.
But instead I hug my heat bag in a heap.
It's like a knife stabbing deep inside the pain is
so bad.
 I hate thinking of others going through it makes
me feel sad.
Aniexty and depression have a big part to play
too.
Endometriosis literally takes over you.
You may run me down and bring me to tears
You may of tortured me over the years.
But one thing you will never do is win
Because I'm a fighter and I'm not giving in.
I will beat you watch and see
Because endo you won't define me!

Dreamland

Dreams are hundreds of thoughts and feelings
put together in your head.
It's where you escape reality when you are
tucked up in your bed.
Some can be amazing and you never want them
to end.
But nightmares also come along where your
fears drive you round the bend.
When I sleep I can get messages from loved
ones no longer here.
I class it as a gift to be their listening ear.
I hope it brings some comfort to those I give
messages to along the way.
To know their loved ones watching over them
and never went away

My baby girl

A poem I wrote for my daughter 🖤🖤🖤 Chloe
my baby girl my beautiful daughter my best
friend
We have a bond that will never end.
When you hurt I feel it too.
I want to protect you in all that you do.
We finish each other sentences, we laugh so
hard we cry.
And if one of us are sad the other one will know
exactly why.
We dream the same dreams and love the same
things.
If we were butterflies we would have matching
wings.
If someone has hurt us the other is ready for
heads to swing.
We are a little bit crazy and we love to sing.

Nanny's little cherubs

A poem I wrote about my grandchildren
🩶🩶🩶🩶

I love being a nanny it brings me so much joy
First a little girl followed by a boy
I never thought I'd get that feeling again of love
I had with your mum.
But you came into my life and that loving
feeling instantly begun.
Your little hands fitted mine just like a glove.
The angels were watching over me knowing I
needed little ones to love.
When I knew I couldn't have any more children
of my own.
My heart felt empty I felt all alone.
I still had so much love to give but it was taken
away from me.
But mummy had you two and it was like it was
ment to be.
I treasure each time you wrap your arms around
me and say I love you
You fixed my broken heart you were my glue.
I will tell you lots of stories and sing you
lullaby's
I will pick you up if you fall.
And wipe your tears if you cry.

I will love you more with each day that goes by.
Because you are the apple of Nannie's eye.
I will bake cakes with you and play your
favourite game.
I will put your photos up in pretty little frames.
And if you have a nightmare and think that
monsters are under your bed.
Nanny will protect you like she always said.

A fairy kiss

If you listen carefully when the moon's in the sky.
You might catch a glimpse of the fairies as they fly.
They dance on the stars as they twinkle so bright.
And blow kisses to everyone wishing them goodnight.
They wear the prettiest flowers in their hair.
And the queen of the fairies sits in her magical chair.
They have tiny cups and saucers as they sip their tea.
And rock there babies on their knees.
They sing beautiful songs and the birds join in too.
Fairyland is full of magic where dreams come true.
Wings made of glitter as pretty as can be.
And they all live in the magical tree.
So if you look out the window and they blow you a kiss.
That's the fairy granting a wish

Fierce

I hide behind a smile but can you really see me?
I'm strong because I've had to be.
I'm fierce and I'm loyal until the end.
I'm definitely better to have as a friend.
But I hurt and I cry I have emotions too.
It's just that I'm made of superglue.
I rise to the challenge come what may.
And live to fight another day.
I am bold, I am beautiful, I am strong.
I write the lyrics to my own survivor song.

A Nans love

Everything seemed so much more magical when
you was here.
Your warmth and kindness pap one too many
beers.
I have so many fond childhood memories I tuck
away.
There's a little place within my heart where you
will always stay.
Everyday without you since you had to go
Its like summer without sunshine and winter
without snow.
But your in a better place now where the sun
will always shine.
Where there is no pain and limited amount of
time.
So this year as I gaze at the wintery sky.
Christmas stars will twinkle and I will know the
reason why

Anything is possible

Stand in front of the mirror look what do you
see?
I see a beautiful woman who can be anything
she wants to be.
A smile that's painted on to make people think
she's ok.
But deep inside her world feels so grey.
Eyes that have cried a thousand tears.
Through empty promises and deepest fears.
But your amazing yes I'm talking to you.
Stop doubting who you are I believe in you I do.
Reach for the stars you can achieve it all .
Be proud of who you are stand tall.

Escapism

Trapped in a bubble of feeling low
Unable to escape no where to go
Consumed with my own thoughts everyday
Wondering if this feeling will ever go away
I see people smiling and the happiness they
show
Show me which way I need to go
I want to get back to that happy place
But this aniexty world is like an endless rat race.
I want to feel liberated and free
I want to release this demon in me.
But what do I do to set him free
Can anyone help and see me?

Forever friends

On this journey many different people will walk in and out of your life.
Some will stay and some will go.
Who's in for the long haul nobody knows.
Friendships will form and stand the test of time
Some will be memories with a bottle of wine.
But those that stand with you through the bad times as well as the good.
Those must be held on to and not misunderstood
You can collect 100 stones until you find that rare gem.
That's just like friendships so hold on to them.
The truest of friends will catch you when you fall.
Will answer the phone in middle of the night when you call.
Will wipe away your tears when your feeling sad.
And paint the town red when your feeling bad.

Blessings

I open my heart and let it be free.
Hoping it will let part of be.
I release the burdens the sadness and pain
In hope of sunshine instead of rain
Wash all the negativity away.
And help me feel clear to start a new day.
With gratitude, blessings and a positive outlook
All the start of my very own book

A little girls love

Fairy's and glitter and cute little bows.
Sparkling crowns and pretty painted toes.
Cute little notes and snuggles in bed.
Imaginary friends made up in your head.
Walking around in mummy's shoes
Magic medicine when you get a bruise.
Secrets you share to never be told.
A little girls love as pure as gold

A little boys love

Sticky fingers on the wall
Playing kick around with a ball
Collecting jars of bugs
Giving mummy loving hugs.
Getting dirty in the mud
Playing with bubbles in the tub.
All these things are what bring me joy
I'm so thankful for my little boy.

What is love?

Love is butterflies in the pit of your tummy.
Love is priceless it's no sum of money.
Love is holding hands walking side by side.
Love is a roller-coaster journey you both ride.
Love is kisses in the rain
Love is when your feeling sad the other feels the
pain.
Love is what I feel every second I'm with you.
Love is our hearts beating as two.

Best friends

I've got your back you've got mine.
Late night chats over a bottle of wine.
A shoulder to cry on when it's all falling apart.
A reassuring hug to mend a broken heart.
Many pictures taken on nights out.
Thinking we are sexy with our famous duck
pouts.
Best friends forever that sisterhood touch.
Couldn't get rid of you if I wanted to, you know
too much

Endo sisters

Cramps in my tummy I can barely walk.
Don't answer the phone i can't talk.
Pains in my back
Pains in my side
Feels like I want to run away and hide.
Feeling anxious, lonely and depressed.
Don't want to wash can't be bothered to get
dressed.
Feeling so tired I just want to sleep.
But my endo leaves me exhausted in a heap.
Appointments with gynae, pain team too.
Endless times what more can they do?.
I feel like I'm fighting you on my own.
I feel like I'm a prisoner in my home.
I try to make plans but end up cancelling on
friends.
Will this nightmare ever end.
Just because you can't see it, it's very much
there.
My tummy swells so bad I don't know what to
wear.
Sitting at home with nothing to do
I login on Facebook and came across you.
Endo support group with people all over the
world.

Just wanting to get their voice heard.
Suddenly I don't feel alone I'm surrounded by you.
All in the same boat not knowing what to do.
Because of you my days don't feel dark anymore.
My endo sisters have opened a loving door.

Christmas eve

Twas the night before Christmas and excitement
filled the air.
Children knew santa Claus would soon be there.
Ella had received her special gift and prepared it
before bed.
She wanted to know santa and the reindeers
would be well fed.
She took out her bottle and filled it with drink.
Santa will need this he will be thirsty I think.
Her magic dust was put on the table as well.
It sparkled and glistened and looked really swell.
The magic helps the reindeers fly
What a great view up in the sky.
Reindeer food was put out too.
Ella was smart she knew what to do.
A cookie for santa to fill up his tum.
He sure has a lot to get done.
A magic key and a note to say.
Thankyou Santa for making my day

Wrapped up winter

The twigs have fallen the tree's are bare.
A carpet of leaves and cold misty air.
The paths glisten like a glittery sheet.
Our park bench is an empty seat.
Children wrapped up nice and snug.
Everyone loves a winter hug.
Tree's decorated with baubles and lights.
Got chocolate and marshmallows for a cosy
night.
Pj's, slippers and festive mince pies.
Seeing the excitement in the childrens eyes.
Christmas is a magical time of the year.
But what makes it special is the people we hold
dear.
It's not about how much you spend.
It's about creating memories with family and
friends.

Recipe of smiles

Add one large hug
Some cracker jokes stirred in a mug.
Sprinkle some love and care.
Then simple add your favourite teddy bear.
Two reassuring hands to hold.
One blanket when your feeling cold.
A cup of your favourite tea.
And this special poem made by me

9 789358 316292